Teens Who Make a Difference in Rural Communities

Youth Outreach Organizations and Community Action

Title List

Teens Who Make a Difference in Rural Communities

Youth Outreach Organizations and Community Action

by Jean Otto Ford

Mason Crest Publishers

Philadelphia

Mason Crest Publishers Inc.
370 Reed Road
Broomall, Pennsylvania 19008
(866) MCP-BOOK (toll free)
www.masoncrest.com

First printing
1 2 3 4 5 6 7 8 9 10
ISBN 978-1-4222-0011-7 (series)

Library of Congress Cataloging-in-Publication Data

Ford, Jean (Jean Otto)
  Teens who make a difference in rural communities : youth outreach organizations and community action / by Jean Otto Ford.
      p. cm. — (Youth in rural North America)
  Includes index.
  ISBN 978-1-4222-0013-1
  1. Rural youth—United States. 2. Community organization—United States. 3. Social action—United States. I. Title. II. Series.
  HQ796.F697 2007
  362.7083'0973—dc22

                                    2005032433

Cover and interior design by MK Bassett-Harvey.
Produced by Harding House Publishing Service, Inc.
www.hardinghousepages.com

Cover image design by Peter Spires Culotta.
Cover photography by iStock Photography (Roberta Osborne, Nancy Nehring, and Lisa F. Young).
Printed in Malaysia by Phoenix Press.

Contents

Introduction

by Celeste Carmichael

Results of a survey published by the Kellogg Foundation reveal that most people consider growing up in the country to be idyllic. And it's true that growing up in a rural environment does have real benefits. Research indicates that families in rural areas consistently have more traditional values, and communities are more closely knit. Rural youth spend more time than their urban counterparts in contact with agriculture and nature. Often youth are responsible for gardens and farm animals, and they benefit from both their sense of responsibility and their understanding of the natural world. Studies also indicate that rural youth are more engaged in their communities, working to improve society and local issues. And let us not forget the psychological and aesthetic benefits of living in a serene rural environment!

The advantages of rural living cannot be overlooked—but neither can the challenges. Statistics from around the country show that children in a rural environment face many of the same difficulties that are typically associated with children living in cities, and they fare worse than urban kids on several key indicators of positive youth development. For example, rural youth are more likely than their urban counterparts to use drugs and alcohol. Many of the problems facing rural youth are exacerbated by isolation, lack of jobs (for both parents and teens), and lack of support services for families in rural communities.

When most people hear the word "rural," they instantly think "farms." Actually, however, less than 12 percent of the population in rural areas make their livings through agriculture. Instead, service jobs are the top industry in rural North America. The lack of opportunities for higher paying jobs can trigger many problems: persistent poverty, lower educational standards, limited access to health care, inadequate housing, underemployment of teens, and lack of extracurricular possibilities. Additionally, the lack of—or in some cases surge of—diverse populations in rural communities presents its own set of challenges for youth and communities. All these concerns lead to the greatest threat to rural communities: the mass exodus of the post–high school population. Teens relocate for educational, recreational, and job opportunities, leaving their hometown indefinitely deficient in youth capital.

This series of books offers an in-depth examination of both the pleasures and challenges for rural youth. Understanding the realities is the first step to expanding the options for rural youth and increasing the likelihood of positive youth development.

CHAPTER 1
Analyzing Activism: The Wallop of One

"You must be the change you wish to see in the world."

—Mahatma Gandhi (1869–1948), spiritual leader who developed and advanced the idea of nonviolent disobedience in India

Jim (Nova Scotia, Canada)

In 2002, Jim was a teenager when he moved to Whycocomagh, a sleepy village in Nova Scotia's Iverness County, the northernmost tip of the peninsula–province. Having a population density much less than the province's average of fifty inhabitants per square mile (about 18 per square kilometer), Whycocomagh residents could immediately spot a "new kid." What they couldn't see was how much this new teen would change their community for good.

No point in Nova Scotia is more than thirty-five miles (56 kilometers) from the sea, yet Iverness County is primarily agricultural. Fifty years of farming advancements had put many smaller local farms out of business, as it has across North America. What struck Jim most was the *number* of abandoned farms in the area. These all-too-frequent sights stirred something in him, and he knew he needed to help revive his new community.

Jim searched government agriculture data, public records, books, the media, farm-organization newsletters, press releases, and information on award recipients for any successful **revitalization** projects already in place in Canada. He studied them—what worked, what didn't—then took what he considered to be the best five approaches and combined them into one effort, the first such cooperative **initiative** in the nation.

In its simplest form, Jim's method encourages landowners, farmers, agricultural processors, restaurant owners, and consumers to work together in a system that mutually promotes farm products and adds value to every step along the way—from soil to table. The theory made sense on paper, but it couldn't work without local support and involvement. Knocking on doors and tirelessly making proposals, Jim obtained just that, and many of those abandoned farms are operating once again.

Jim's efforts earned him the 2004 First Young Leaders in Rural Canada Award (in innovation), a national award sponsored by Canada's Rural Secretariat. Broken farmland and the initiative of one compassionate, motivated teen: that's all it took in Nova Scotia to transform an entire farming community.

Canada's abandoned farms may look picturesque, but they are signs of an ailing rural economy. Jim's efforts helped transform many of Nova Scotia's old farms so that they are once more producing both food and money for this rural area.

Emily (Georgia, United States)

Many people think only of New York, Toronto, Hollywood, or other urban centers when they think "performance art." It never occurs to them that the arts can thrive in pockets of rural America. Consider Bartow County, Georgia, thanks to teenage 4-H member and arts-enthusiast Emily.

By definition, Bartow County, where Emily lives, is rural. According to the 2000 Census, just over 76,000 people share the wide valleys and steep ridges that characterize this 471-square-mile

Emily helped enrich the lives of others by bringing the performing arts to her town.

(1,220-square-kilometer) river basin. That's just 161 people per square mile (62 per square kilometer).

Nearly three times as many residents (16,676) here receive a high school education (or less) as those who go on to receive four-year degrees (4,751), and over two-thirds of Bartow residents have never lived anywhere but Georgia. Still, despite lacking the obvious exposure and resources metropolitan areas offer, Emily believes the arts are as much for "country folk" as for urban dwellers, and she's doing something about it.

While attending National 4-H Congress in 2003, Emily saw what other 4-H members were doing and wondered, why couldn't she?

Local kids needed things to do; the Boys' and Girls' Clubs needed programs; Emily loved the arts, and that was already her project area in 4-H. She explains in a *4-H USA* article, "I have received so much just being involved in the performing arts—socially, emotionally, and intellectually. I, along with a group of my peers, feel that it is now time to begin giving back to our community."

To Emily, the means of giving back was obvious: a program engaging local children in the arts. Her brainchild, Performing Arts for Community Kids (PACK), was the result. The official purpose of Emily's PACK program is "to educate and enrich the lives of children (ages five to twelve) in the arts, and to provide a fun project-club in which they can learn about different art forms, be creative, and express and develop talents." Emily and her team of five other Bartow County 4-H members now volunteer-teach five local classes ranging from dance to drama to musical theater, rotating each monthly. These teens are reaching one child at a time.

Emily's efforts could gain national recognition, not to mention a *4-H USA* $10,000 prize. (To learn more about 4-H, see chapter 4.) A community was lacking something; one girl had a passion and acted on it. That's all it took in rural Georgia.

Defining "Making a Difference"

Two very different teens noticed two very different needs and changed two very different communities forever. In both cases, entire communities benefited, but the impact started with one average teenager who saw a need. These examples show communitywide needs, but kids respond to individual needs, too, and impacting even one life makes a difference.

Unfortunately, many teens hear stories like these and think that unless their impact is just as widespread or just as publicly

Language Lay-Down

Some teenagers (and adults) fear "getting involved" because they have negative associations with the concept. To clarify, here are a few words people encounter when lending a hand.

action: An act of will; a thing done.

activism: A practice emphasizing direct vigorous action in support of one side of an issue.

activist: Someone who engages in direct vigorous action in support of one side of an issue.

charity: Goodwill toward or love of humanity; generosity and helpfulness, especially toward the needy or suffering; an organization that engages in charity.

cause: A principle or movement defended or supported by an individual or group; a charitable undertaking.

recognized, it's less significant. Others hear the words "activism," "activist," "charity," "cause," or even "outreach" and mistakenly think "*radicals*" or at least some extreme action. Worse, some kids think they couldn't possibly do anything to help anyone, especially if they live in the middle of nowhere, far from city resources.

Making a difference, however, simply involves choosing to do something to impact an issue about which you feel strongly—and then doing it. Each person on this planet has something to give, community: A unified body of individuals; an interacting population of various kinds of individuals in a common location; broadly, the area itself.

community action: A thing done by an act of will to benefit a body of individuals with something in common (belief, ethnicity, location, etc.).

outreach: The act of extending services or assistance beyond usual limits.

volunteer: A person who willingly undertakes an act of service.

volunteerism: The practice of doing volunteer work in community service.

<u>Source</u>: Merriam-Webster's Collegiate Dictionary, 10th edition.

something to contribute; taking action usually costs nothing more than time and energy. Not every action needs to be long term, dramatic, complex, or militant. In fact, some of the most profound acts of service are also the simplest.

This book spotlights rural kids whose good deeds all across North America have impacted individuals, towns, counties, states, provinces, nations, and even the world. Their motivation generally wasn't material reward or recognition, although the sense of

The more we work together, the greater the
outcome of our good deeds.

Shattering the Stereotype

Young people across the continent are impacting lives in record numbers. See for yourself:

- Canadian youth account for 15 percent of all volunteer hours in their country, totaling 154 million volunteer hours per year.

- U.S. teenagers (ages sixteen to nineteen) account for over 186 million volunteer hours for their country and for 16 percent of all U.S. volunteers.

- Fifty-eight percent of Canadian teens (ages fifteen through nineteen), and 70 percent of young adults (ages twenty to twenty-four) gave a total of $308 million to charity during the year 2000. Over 50 percent also gave food or clothing.

- In 2000, the dollar value of services carried out on National Youth Service Day (U.S.) alone exceeded $171 million. That's just one day of kids in action!

satisfaction was often huge. Nor did these kids get involved because the work was easy.

Support programs and resources abound if you know where to look, but perhaps the greatest single resource for "making a difference" is the human spirit—the drive of a single soul committed to impacting even one life for good. And that happens in rural areas just as often as in urban, among young people as often as older ones.

Myth Busters

- More Americans live rurally than most people think: one-fifth (20 percent) of U.S. residents and one-third (33 percent) of Canadians live in officially defined rural areas.

- Most rural teens are not farmers. In fact, only 6.3 percent of rural families live on farms.

Defining "Rural"

Many people misunderstand rural North America. For example, one poll found the majority of U.S. residents think rural regions are usually agricultural, yet, according to the National Advisory Committee on Rural Social Services, only 6.3 percent of rural Americans live on farms. Others picture rural towns as safe, happy havens characterized by unlocked doors and pies cooling in open windows. However, rural crime and substance-abuse rates are fast approaching—and in some cases passing—those of North American cities. Popular assumptions of picture-postcard prosperity frequently downplay or deny heartbreaking struggles of rural poverty. Clearly, rural North America faces many of the same challenges as urban centers.

Stereotypes about what it means to be rural are everywhere, and, like all stereotypes, they rarely depict what's real. Many differences among and within North America's rural communities prevent generalizing the people and their environments. Even the term "rural" defies specific definition. North America's remote regions are simply too diverse for one adjective.

Many people have stereotypes about people who live in the country. They assume that all people in rural areas look and act a certain way. Some of these stereotypes may be positive—like assuming that all people who live in the country are simple, honest folk. Others are more negative, like thinking that rural residents are ignorant louts with mullets and scraggly beards. The reality is that people who live in the country are as different from one another as people who live in more urban areas.

Government agencies look to two main characteristics when officially determining if a region is rural: how remote (or how far away) an area is from other population centers and low population density (the number of residents per square mile). For example, the U.S. Census Bureau defines "rural" as any one area with a population density of less than 1,000 people per square mile that's also surrounded by census "blocks" with densities fewer than 500 people per square mile. The Office of Management and Budget defines its rural equivalent (termed "non-metropolitan") as counties "outside the boundaries of metropolitan areas and having no cities with as many as 50,000 residents." Whether using remoteness or density, both measures are relevant when classifying rural-ness.

According to the USDA Economic Research Association, "rural" U.S. regions span over 2,052 counties, contain 75 percent of all U.S. soil, and house nearly one-fifth of the country's population. National Libraries and Archives Canada reports one-third of Canadians live in rural and remote areas. Think of the differences in climate and geography across these two nations. Think of the varying natural resources and peoples.

Take any two, average rural communities: a prosperous fishing village in Newfoundland and an impoverished mountain town of central Appalachia. How can they compare? Now examine a stable shantytown along the Rio Grande or a working farm community in the Midwest. Then consider the *Aboriginal* village in Manitoba or an American Indian reservation in South Dakota. These places might all technically be "rural," but that's where their similarity ends.

Neither geography nor people groups, neither occupation nor lifestyle can paint rural America with one sweeping brushstroke. That goes for rural youth, too. And just like in urban and suburban areas, some teens choose to make a difference in their worlds regardless of obstacles or circumstances. Taking action is not a matter of region as much as it is a matter of heart.

Rural Youth and Activism

Rural youth do face challenges unique to isolation, lack of technology, and distance from city resources, but the obstacles they face are not necessarily any more or less challenging than those of their urban counterparts—just different. And with such variety among rural communities, individual and community needs are bound to be diverse. This means that the opportunities to get involved are many and varied.

Washing cars is a fun way to help raise money for charity.

Hot Spots for Helping

Where exactly do North American teens volunteer?

<u>United States</u> (volunteers ages sixteen through nineteen):

34.9 percent	educational or youth services
31.3 percent	religious/ministry work
11.5 percent	social or community organizations
6.9 percent	hospitals or other health care facilities
4.4 percent	civic/political/international organizations or causes
3.5 percent	sports/hobby/cultural organizations or causes
2.6 percent	other groups
1.4 percent	environmental/animal care/ humane societies
1.2 percent	public safety services
remaining	didn't provide information

Look at the statistics. According to the 2004 Bureau of Labor Statistics report "Volunteering in the U.S.," over 29 percent of all teens ages sixteen through nineteen volunteered in some way in 2004. Canada's National Survey of Giving, Volunteering, and Participating 2000 reports that 37 percent of Canadian youth ages

Canada (volunteers ages fifteen through nineteen)*:

22.0 percent   social service organizations
                       (religious or secular)

19.0 percent   education and research

18.0 percent   art/culture/recreation

*This survey listed only the top three areas of service.

Sources: The Bureau of Labor Statistics 2004 report "Volunteering in the United States" and Canada's "National Survey of Giving, Volunteering, and Participating 2000."

fifteen through nineteen gave their time and talents in some capacity that year. An overwhelming majority (75 percent) of these teens worked for just one cause, but the types of organizations for which they worked varied as much as the kids surveyed. (The U.S. survey categorized where teens served into ten broad groups, while the Canada survey reported the top three general areas.)

The following chapters illustrate just a few of the opportunities for making a mark in this world. Whether touching the international community or a solitary soul, each case study bears testimony to "the power of one." Remember: anyone, anywhere, of any age, in any life circumstance can make a difference, even kids from rural communities. These stories show how ordinary rural youth with extraordinary hearts came to impact their worlds far and near.

CHAPTER 2
Helping Hearth and Home: Profiles of Local Impact

"Don't mourn, organize."

—Mary Harris "Mother" Jones (1830–1920), early twentieth-century activist known for championing miners' rights and fighting the evils of child labor

Hope (Kentucky, United States)

At sixteen, Hope attended the sole remaining community school in mountainous Knott County, Kentucky. Her home village of Lotts Creek was miles from the nearest business or store. Much to her dismay, coal mining was still wreaking havoc on the environment of Kentucky's mountains, particularly one creek that ran near her house.

Hope is a self-proclaimed activist. In Save the Children's 2002 "Voices of Rural Children and Youth: The Power of Activism," she explains:

> I'm proud to be an activist. . . . I've realized you don't have to be an adult to be an activist and to make a difference.
>
> I started becoming involved in the Number 4 coal issue when I was fifteen years old. A man from the Kentuckians for the Commonwealth came to our school trying to . . . stop a permit that gave the Diamond Mae Coal Company authority to mine Kelly Fork. I was aware of the water issue but never thought that, as a kid, I could do much about it. Finding out that I had a voice and that I could make a difference gave me a whole new way to view my life.
>
> Kelly Fork is right above my house, and I have lots of friends who live there. Since the Diamond Mae Coal Company came in to mine Kelly Fork, bad things have been happening to our entire community.
>
> I became an activist because I see and smell our water and because I know that we can't drink this water. Oh gosh, on any given day we can turn on our faucets and sometimes the water is crystal clear. Other days it looks gray and dingy, and other days there is so much oil in it that it's completely purple or even black. Because of mining, our water tables have shifted. We used to have white sulfur and now we have red sulfur. It smells like rotten eggs—it's really, really nasty. It's so foul that when we turn on our faucets, we often have to leave the room.
>
> The coal company doesn't care that we can't drink our water or even bathe in our water. They don't have to look at it, or smell it, or drink it. They don't even have to drive long distances just to buy bottled water. After all, isn't water supposed to be free and available to all people? Just because we are poor and from the mountains, aren't we entitled to clean water? I know that mining puts a lot of people to work in our area and it is our biggest industry, but can't the coal companies have some consideration for the people who live on or near the mountain?

Coal mines take a heavy toll on the communities that live near them. One teenager realized she had the power to make a difference.

I was disturbed when I first heard about the Number 4 coal issue, and I got it in my head that maybe me and my friends could make a difference. With help from one of my teachers, we organized a protest and got a bus to take us to Frankfort to fight this battle. I'm an outspoken girl, and I never really knew what a powerful voice I had. We came to Frankfort prepared with signs, chants, and bottles of dirty water we got from our own faucets . . . we didn't know what to expect. There were news people all over the place . . . I just wanted to crawl back on that bus. I was so nervous. I didn't crawl back because everyone was looking to me as their leader.

We started chanting. . . . We got out our signs and banners. I got out my jar of water that looked like it had three inches of oil in it. . . . Finally a man who worked for the Department of Surface Mining invited us in. He told us that there was not much that could be done—that the mining . . . would continue.

I became very upset. I felt like my chest was caving in. I took a few deep breaths and asked again if he would hold the permit and help us. He told us that he was sorry, that he couldn't do that. . . . We were teens and were trying desperately to help our community. Yet even our government would not help.

In the end, the Diamond Mae Coal Company promised they would provide money to pipe city water into Kelly Fork. Although we couldn't stop the mining, we felt a victory knowing that at least we would get clean water.

Something really good came out of all this. As kids we learned that we could work together as a unified force to make change. You can be just one voice and your one little voice can make a big difference.

One Appalachian teen with the help of one teacher organized forty youths and twelve adults to march in protest and fight for something they deeply believed was right. That one voice triggered fifty-two more, and fifty-two caught the attention of the press, the government, and mining company officials. Life in Lotts Creek and Kelly Fork is very different today because of the willingness of one teen to act.

The Appalachian Mountains, where both Hope and Isaac live, have some of the most remote rural areas in the United States.

Isaac (Kentucky, United States)

Imagine a several-miles-long, wooded hollow carved by mountain streams. A single gravel road follows the natural gorge, connecting a handful of homes dotting its forests. This Kentucky street, if you can call it that, has no street signs; it's the street where Isaac grew up.

The village of Cowan is the nearest "town." That's where the Cowan Community Center is, the center where Isaac now volunteers for AmeriCorps*VISTA (Volunteers in Service to America). It is also the center where, at age eleven, he first got involved in a youth group.

Rural teens—like all teenagers—are always looking for something to do. Community service projects offer them opportunities to channel their energies.

In "Voices of Rural Children and Youth: Promise Uncovered," a 2002 report by Save the Children, Isaac wrote:

All my brothers and sisters were involved also, and this had a big impact on my family. Many kids growing up in this area are very shy. That's how I used to be. I could barely talk to people and look them in the eye. I had no self-confidence. Everyone here grows up feeling self-conscious about being from Eastern Kentucky. I knew all the stereotypes people had about me and my people. I've learned that it's not bad to be a hillbilly, and I'm proud of my background. My experience with youth group pushed me into situations where I learned that I had ideas and opinions and that it was okay to express them. I discovered that I had a powerful voice.

Like most rural teens, when Isaac first joined a youth group at age eleven, he was looking for something to do. But over his years at the center, he grew—in confidence, in knowledge, and in his passion to give something back to his community. The individual volunteers who invested in Isaac helped this once-insecure boy discover his value, develop his skills, and realize his potential. They simply encouraged and equipped him, then set him loose. The encouraged became the encourager. The boy who was led became a leader.

After a few years, I became a leader in the youth group and eventually its president. As president, I learned how to facilitate meetings and help develop our team. We did several community service projects, such as cleaning up the rivers throughout our community. Save the Children provided us with funding to go to a statewide leadership training conference. . . . Through this training we became more aware of our community issues and more empowered to try new things to improve our communities. We learned that regardless of what we learn, we are the only ones who can truly help ourselves. We can get the best training in the world, but it doesn't matter unless we use it the right way.

Another program that was very valuable to me was Upward Bound. We took trips to D.C., New York City, and Chicago. This

> "When you influence a child, you influence a life. When you influence a parent, you influence a family. . . . When you influence a leader, you influence all who look to him or her for leadership."
>
> —Bobb Biehl, from <u>On My Own Handbook: 100 Secrets of Success to Prepare Young People for Life in the Real World</u>

travel experience was so important in giving me a broader understanding that although places are different, people are basically the same everywhere. We all have the same problems.

If anyone had enormous barriers to getting involved, Isaac did. No public library. No Internet. No money. No transportation. Not even school support. The single resource with any potential was a tiny community center in Cowan, the only place for miles that offered any services (most were free) to children, youth, and adults. How did this rural Appalachian teen take that first step? He walked through the doors.

Tomminea (Mississippi, United States)

"I came back to Marks because . . . I wanted to do something at home," Tomminea explains in "The Voices of Rural Children and Youth" a 2002 article by Save the Children:

> I don't know if I'll be here forever, but I need to do something for my people—for the kids.

Rural schools often lack the money to offer students the same opportunities they might find in suburban schools.

But this is hard because all the people who go to college around here, they leave immediately and no one actually comes back. . . . I can't count any of my classmates who went to college who are here. But I want to be here.

Rural activism faces a unique challenge because so many teenagers abandon their local areas for urban centers. Employment and educational choices vary widely in cities and are generally more available. Plus the pay is better, and the schools are often better. Consequently, a lot of sixteen-, seventeen-, and eighteen-year-olds leave rural America to get jobs or college degrees and never return.

Sociologists call this problem the "brain drain," because it is often youths with the greatest potential who leave to gain experience or education and never return. That "drains" the local community of perhaps its most valuable resource: its young people—their fresh ideas, energy, and talent. Tomminea wasn't one of those teens who left forever.

Tomminea is unusual. After leaving for college, she came back to her hometown to work as a youth coordinator for Quitman County Development Organization. (AmeriCorps*VISTA supports her work.) The extent to which she is willing to put others' needs above her own is inspiring. And it has cost her a great deal.

"God knows . . . there are so many other things I want to do with my life," Tomminea continues. "I'd love to get a job working for a magazine. I'd love to go to New York. My uncle always tells me that it's hard to get people to forgo the riches of the world. Yet the thing that is keeping me here is the kids."

Deep down, Tomminea believes the sacrifice she's making is worth it. This young woman is making a difference. With the support of a national organization, a local girl is impacting her rural community one life at a time. She's changing lives, and that's rewarding:

> I think that these kids listen to me and hear what I say. I recently had a conversation with a twelve-year-old girl who told me that her best friend was pregnant. We talked, and I told her about my life and that if I had a child, I couldn't have done any of the things that I've done. I think she heard me.
>
> There's no one else doing what I'm doing for these kids. I love these kids. . . . And they need so much. We have a program here, but there are only so many kids that we can handle. And there's really no other place for them to go. They relate to me because I'm young and they think I'm different. I listen to the same music that they do, and I guess I'm a good role model.
>
> Some of the girls tell me they want to be just like me. This is why it's so hard to leave. I often just sit and cry. . . . So many of the little girls around here get pregnant. I'm convinced it's because they have nothing else to do. I just think that if they had something else to do and someone to tell them that it hurts you to get pregnant, then maybe it would be different.

Teenagers can be powerful leaders for their peers, because young adults often relate better to others their own age.

One rural, hometown girl saw how much younger kids were struggling in her community, so she decided to postpone her plans and help them. Author Bobb Biehl once said, "If you impact a child, you impact a life." That's what Tomminea is doing, and her local community is slowly changing, one life at a time.

Teenage pregnancy is an all-too common occurrence in many rural communities.

Unique Passions

All people experience their communities uniquely, so what strikes one person as an urgent need may not strike another at all. Some may not even see any problem. That's why our communities need each and every one of us, with our separate sensitivities, and why we need each other.

Take, for instance, the opening examples in this chapter. Two young women and one young man saw three distinct problems impacting their regions and chose to do something about them. The first turned to her school and her own resources; the second volunteered at his community center through a national organization, AmeriCorps*VISTA; and the third returned to her village as an AmeriCorps*VISTA employee and counselor.

Hope entered community activism at fifteen. Isaac was only eleven when he first joined his community's youth group; by his mid-teens he was a leader; and by seventeen he was volunteer staff at the same community center. Tomminea was already college-age when she began her work. Environmental and health issues drove Hope, and she gathered others around her to support her cause. Compassion and children's needs drove both Isaac and Tomminea, and both sought the support of established organizations, yet Isaac was part of a community center and worked with groups of boys, and Tomminea largely worked one-on-one, alone.

There are countless ways of making a local difference. No single guidebook exists on the "who, what, where, when, and why" of community action, but there is a common first step: paying attention. Nearly every case where rural youth impact their communities first involves simply noticing what's going on. Here are three examples:

- Eddie is the teenage son of former migrant workers. He also happens to be a baseball fanatic. One day he noticed that the local migrant children just sat around on dusty stoops after school. They really needed something to do. Eddie, who played right field for his high school baseball team, decided to act on what he saw. Using equipment borrowed mostly from his friends and money borrowed from his family, Eddie set up a free baseball camp for migrant children whose parents work as fruit and vegetable pickers in nearby fields. Every year since 2001, Eddie's camp has run several week-long programs for these kids. Now they spend much of their free time playing baseball. One added bonus: many youth credit Eddie's program with keeping them from the drugs and gang activity that plague the area.

• While doing research for a history project, students from a rural South Carolina middle school noticed one seemingly insignificant fact buried in their data. Apparently a former Confederate soldier from South Carolina, in response to New York City's generous 1867 gift of a fire wagon (to replace fire equipment his town had lost in the Civil War), pledged that the state would return the kindness "should misfortune ever befall the Empire City." When the students read of the promise, tragedy had befallen New York City on September 11, 2001, and no one had yet kept the soldier's pledge. These eleven- to thirteen-year-olds determined to honor their ancestor's promise. They wrote to New York firefighters to learn how they could best help, launched a campaign to raise enough money to cover the cost of a new fire engine (more than $345,000), and achieved their goal within two months. New York has one more fire engine because of these kids, and a southern community has the satisfaction of knowing it did the right thing.

• After attending a holiday party for local foster kids, Jaclyn walked away thinking, *I could do better*. Her heart broke for her little foster brother. (Jaclyn is not a foster child herself, but her family hosts foster children.) The party had no Santa, no Christmas music, no stockings, and no toys. So, with the help of her parents, the eleven-year-old set up her nonprofit organization Jaclyn's Wish to make foster children's holiday wishes come true. Every year since, she has taken donations and worked hard to throw a celebration worthy of the children and holiday it celebrates.

When everyone contributes, everyone benefits.

Many preteens might have read the soldier's promise to New York and moved on, never making the connection between September 11 and the conditions of the pledge. Another teenager might have driven right by migrant kids sitting on their stoops and never given them a second glance. (Countless numbers already had.) Most teens would have noticed the lack of Santa and presents at the foster kids' party, and a few might have even felt bad for the children, but only one moved beyond noticing to action.

No matter how big the
problem, one small person
can make a difference!

Putting Your Money Where Your Mouth Is

"Noticing" isn't enough. These rural young people did see the problems, but then each one also gathered information and brainstormed how best to help. Yet, even noticing *and* having information or a plan is not enough. By definition, activists act. They must *do* something, too.

The South Carolina students launched a campaign. That means they must have made up and posted flyers; they likely held fund-raisers; and they certainly talked with people. As the money came in, someone had to track it, send receipts, and ultimately distribute what they raised to a grateful group of New York firefighters. These kids desired to help, found a way, and *did something*.

Eddie gathered any equipment he could scrounge up. He borrowed what he could and used some of his own. He talked with adults in the migrant-children's community and told them what he'd like to do. He borrowed some money from his mom and dad to print flyers and buy miscellaneous supplies. He set up times and dates, and he got a few friends to help coach. Then he worked with the kids.

Jaclyn and her parents found out how to create a nonprofit charity and did so. Then, throughout the year, they collected donations for her Christmas party. Each fall, Jaclyn pulled things together. She found and reserved a place, figured out how many foster children could potentially come and who they were (at least ages and gender), purchased decorations, hired a Santa, arranged for music and refreshments, and gathered and wrapped enough presents for each child to have at least one. Finally, just before the party, she set up and decorated. Impacting those foster kids took action.

All three attempts at affecting change in these cases were successful because passion, knowledge, *and action*—heart, head, *and hands*—were there. Remember, you can "notice" and "feel" all you want, but both are meaningless without appropriate action. And at the same time, you can "act" all you want, too, but if actions aren't based on strategic knowledge and if they lack heart, what you do will likely prove as fruitless as taking no action at all. The greatest chance for impact depends on inspiration, information, and action each being present.

Local Action via Established Organizations

Young people often see needs adults miss, and most genuinely believe they can do something about what they see. In fact, according to Princeton's "Do Something Young People's Involvement Survey," 73 percent of teens living in the United States believe they can make a difference in their communities. The problem is many don't know how or where to begin.

One of the best ways to get started is to join an existing community-service group. Many local groups—whether accessible through school, church, or the community—already have resources in place and know the ins and outs of impacting the area; taking that first step with someone who's experienced is usually less intimidating. Plus, by definition, groups divide tasks among many hands, so "getting involved" can start small and be less overwhelming. Boys' and Girls' Clubs of America, 4-H, scouts, and faith-based youth programs are great examples of established groups. Seeing what others have done or are doing can spark ideas.

Two cases we've covered so far illustrate young people who chose to help via established organizations: this chapter's Tomminea (rural-teen pregnancy and youth counseling via AmeriCorps*VISTA) and Emily from chapter 1 (performing arts for rural kids via 4-H). Most high schools, including rural ones, also offer general, well-defined, citizenship clubs like National Honor Society and issue-oriented clubs like Students Against Drunk Driving (SADD).

Community outreach programs vary from school to school, even among schools within the same district, but high school clubs all across North America are bettering their immediate localities in a multitude of ways: picking up trash, visiting the elderly, collecting and distributing food, investing in local children, reaching out to the

Often, it takes many hands to accomplish a big goal for the greater good.

handicapped, sheltering the poor, championing the environment, educating on health and safety issues, teaching others to read, and so on. Opportunities are countless, but a number of well-established, community-service-oriented, youth organizations can help you get started. Here are a few of the most common. (Contact information is listed in the back of the book.)

- Best Buddies

- Big Brothers/Big Sisters

- Boy Scouts of America

- Boys' and Girls' Clubs of America

- Boys' and Girls' Clubs of Canada

- 4-H Canada

- 4-H USA

- Girl Guides (Canada)

- Girl Scouts of the U.S.A.

- Interact Clubs (Youth Rotary)

- Key Clubs International (Youth Kiwanis)

- Leo Clubs (Youth Lions)

- National Honor Society

- Scouting Canada

- SADD (Students Against Drunk Driving)

- YAD (Youth Against Drugs)

- YMCA

Such student clubs across the continent are tackling issues as diverse as the environment, discrimination (including gay/lesbian, the disabled, various ethnicities, and religions), homelessness, hunger, poverty, substance abuse, illiteracy, and animal rights. It all depends on the community, student interest, and the availability of adult supervisors.

If your school doesn't offer any of these programs, start one! Contact the club's national, state, provincial, or county chapter. Most have Web sites or 800 numbers, and representatives there can guide you. (Details about some of these organizations are spotlighted through this book.)

Local Action on Your Own

Some students encounter needs that require independent action. In this chapter we've seen four examples of local activism without the benefit of established organizations: environment and health (Hope), migrant workers' children (Eddie), historical debt/local integrity (South Carolina students), and foster children (Jaclyn). Seeing what touched each student and how each one approached the issue can not only inspire others to act, it can provide pointers on how to get the job done.

Despite living in rural, isolated, or depressed communities, the financial cost to each of these youths was minimal if any. They tapped the resources of their schools, families, friends, and the public. They even raised donations. In each case, the greatest cost was time and energy. That's the downside to acting independently: much of the work is on just a few shoulders. The upside is that you don't have to wait on any bureaucracy and can take action your own way.

Remember that pros and cons *saturate* both approaches to local activism. The means of change vary and largely depend on the nature of the issue; the personality, passions, skills, and resources of the activist; and available resources in the region. (For example, if no related program or organization exists in your area, you'll likely have to establish one or champion the cause on your own.) These same factors hold true for regional, state, and provincial activism and outreach.

Spotlight: AmeriCorps

In 1993, U.S. president Bill Clinton signed legislation establishing the Corporation for National and Community Service, bringing a host of community-service programs under one central organization. AmeriCorps is just one program of that corporation and unites three main service organizations: AmeriCorps*State and National, AmeriCorps*VISTA (Volunteers in Service to America, created by President L. B. Johnson in 1964), and AmeriCorps*NCCC (National Civilian Community Corps).

AmeriCorps*State and National provides government-funded financial grants (not loans) to public and nonprofit organizations that sponsor programs across the United States. These programs involve thousands of Americans serving critical community needs in education, health, and the environment. Sample activities might include building homes, restoring parks, mentoring local youth, and assisting crime victims. Faith-based and community organizations, Native American tribes, public service groups, and educational institutions train and place AmeriCorps members. Most placements are temporary, either one year or one summer.

AmeriCorps*VISTA provides full-time, nominally paid personnel to various community organizations to create and build programs geared toward ultimately elevating low-income individuals and families out of poverty. VISTA workers must be at least eighteen years old and serve for at least one year. AmeriCorps*VISTA partners with established organizations and agencies nationwide to fight illiteracy, create business opportunities, increase and improve housing, improve health services, and bring technology to digitally deprived areas.

AmeriCorps*NCCC is a full-time, residential, team-based, ten-month program for young adults ages eighteen to twenty-four. Members live and train on one of five U.S. campuses in California, Colorado, South Carolina, Maryland, or Washington, D.C., then service communities in every state. Each service project typically lasts an intense six to eight weeks and ranges from responding to natural disasters to tutoring students. The mission is to develop America's young adults into leaders while strengthening communities.

CHAPTER 3
Reaching the Region: Profiles of County, State, and Provincial Impact

"The needs you feel strongest about are also the most likely to inspire you."

—Bobb Biehl, from *The On My Own Handbook: 100 Secrets of Success to Prepare Young People for Life in the Real World*

Leonard (Pennsylvania, United States)

When he was just thirteen, Leonard was diagnosed with a cancer that's almost always fatal. By the time he was fourteen, hundreds of tumors had spread throughout his body. Not willing to give up,

Decisions, Decisions

Most U.S. youth volunteers contributed their time to one organization—75 percent—but over 17 percent split their time between two.

his mother Flo took him from his sleepy rural town of Hopbottom to a renowned cancer treatment center in New York City. Mother and son had to stay in nearby Queens for a time to get through daily treatments.

On their way back to Queens one day, Leonard nearly collapsed a block short of the subway. Seeing the forlorn mother and her obviously ill son, a homeless man offered to help them. He picked up their bag and helped the two onto the train. Furthermore, he stayed with them through their stop, and when they got off the subway, he hailed a cab for them and placed the bag in the cab's trunk.

This kind gentleman saw a mother and child needing help and gave it. It was that simple. Leonard and his mom both remember the homeless man's words as she pressed a five-dollar bill into his hand: "Don't abandon me."

Over the next two years, Leonard and his mom regularly returned to the city for follow-up tests and treatment—Leonard miraculously recovered—but they never again saw the man who had helped them. One damp, bone-chilling morning, they noticed one "regular" lying on a street vent bundled up in a bright-pink, crocheted blanket someone had given him so he wouldn't freeze. At that moment, three words came back to haunt them, and they knew what they had to do.

When they returned to tiny, one-flashing-traffic light Hopbottom —population 345—Leonard and his siblings gathered up clothes

The homeless need our help and compassion.

they no longer wore. Leonard's mom went to the barn to gather old sewing supplies she stored there. From his family's discarded jeans, sweats, shirts, and sweaters, plus two, worn tablecloths, Leonard and Flo made their first, handmade "Ugly Quilt," a crude, layered, patchwork sleeping bag.

The next week, the family ventured from their rolling hills into Manhattan to give away that first bag. The gratitude in the shivering recipient's eyes said it all. Within a year, the family had made eight more bags, and with each one they learned something new. They found out that sometimes a homeless parent and child needed to share a bag to keep warm, so dimensions of the bags grew. Neckties became handles to roll and tie the quilts. Finally, they learned the uglier, the better! That way, those receiving a sleeping bag wouldn't be tempted to sell the gift for money.

Making scarves and quilts for the homeless is one way rural teens can contribute to urban communities.

Neighbors learned of the family's work, and word spread throughout the rural county. Before long, bags of donated clothing, sheets, and fabric started turning up on the front porch. Then a local church asked if the family could demonstrate how to make the quilted bags. These were the roots of My Brother's Keeper and Project WARMTH.

Making Ugly Quilts quickly became favorite projects around the region. Church groups, civic clubs, and schools got involved. Middle-school classes stitched quilts for grades. Scouts sewed quilts for merit badges. The Salvation Army and Red Cross even joined the effort by donating materials, and the odd sleeping bags multiplied.

"When the Ugly Quilts are finished, many of them are delivered to our house. As soon as they arrive, we take them to people in New York, Scranton, Philadelphia, and other nearby cities," Leonard explained in one national article. "Last year, we gave out more than 5,300 Ugly Quilts." Flo continues:

> Recently my husband Jim and I were in Manhattan, and we pulled up next to a man holding a cardboard sign that read, "I need food." Jim said to him, "I don't have any food, but do you want a sleeping bag?" The man nodded and motioned for us to follow him around the corner.
>
> We couldn't believe what we saw: an entire *encampment* of homeless men, women, and children. The man asked politely, "Can I give one to my friend?" He walked over to large cardboard box with a wheelchair parked next to it and offered the first bag to his friend, who lived in the box. Then he came back to ask for one for himself. "Can I have that purple one?" he asked. Just having a choice restored his dignity for a moment.

One teenage boy and his mom, a family's heart of compassion, some discarded clothing, a generous farm community, and a bit of time—that's all it took to ultimately bring warmth, perhaps even life, to thousands of homeless people across eastern Pennsylvania and southern New York.

Rena and Jenna (Utah, United States)

Rena had just completed fourth grade when she first saw the pair of marble busts flanking a chamber's entrance when she went with her father to visit the Utah State Capitol. She initially noticed they were American Indian—Rena, too, is Native American—then something about their features caught her attention. Her eyes lit up with recognition: John Duncan, her great-great-grandfather, and Unca Som,

Spotlight: Scouting

Boy Scouts of America and Scouts Canada are both member associations of the World Scout Conference, but neither the United States nor its northern neighbor can claim its origins. Scouting began on Brownsea Island, England, in 1907 from ideas published in a book by Robert Baden-Powell, <u>Scouting for Boys</u>. The book and its methods had universal appeal, and the program quickly spread worldwide. Scouting is now the largest voluntary youth movement in the world, with total membership exceeding 25 million boys and young men ages five to seventeen. (U.S. Boy Scouts alone number over six million, and Scouts Canada cites over 212,000 members.) Although the specific administration of scouting programs might vary slightly from country to country, the entire movement adheres to the same guiding principles of the Scout Promise and Laws and seeks to fulfill the same foundational mission: to prepare young men for adulthood in today's world by instilling scouting values and equipping them to make ethical and moral choices over their lifetimes.

Girl Guides of Canada is an organization for Canadian girls and young women that challenges its members in various areas of personal development while empowering them to be responsible, independent, caring citizens so they can contribute responsibly to their communities. (The aim of the organization has always been to foster good citizenship skills in its members.) Interestingly, the "Girl Guide Movement" originated in England in 1909 when Robert Baden-Powell (Boy Scouts' founder) asked his sister, Agnes Baden-Powell, to help him start an organization for girls. The first official Canadian chapter followed the next year. The movement spread across Canada's provinces by 1912, and in 1917, the Canadian government passed an act of Parliament approving the constitution of the Canadian Girl Guides Association. It is currently the largest organization for girls and young women in Canada, with nearly 110,000 girls ages five through seventeen.

Girl Scouts of the USA is the U.S. equivalent to Girl Guides of Canada. It, too, is dedicated to helping girls and young women everywhere—rural, suburban, or urban—build character and gain success in the real world. With the help of adult volunteers, members are encouraged to develop leadership skills, strong values, and social conscience. Girl Scouts USA began in 1912 in Georgia with just eighteen members. It now boasts nearly four million members spread over 236,000 troops/groups in the United States and its territories. Girl Scouts USA is part of the World Association of Girl Guides and Girl Scouts, an international family of 8.5 million girls spread over 144 countries.

The actions of just two teens can reach as far as local, state, and the federal government.

her great-great-great-grandfather! She recognized them from old family photos. Just to be sure, the excited girl searched for names. She didn't find any. No one had identified either statue.

Most visitors to the capitol at that time assumed the sculptures were anonymous Indians—general representations of Utah's Native American history. To Rena and her father, the nameless portraits were real men. Father and daughter could trace their elders' firm chins and the crows'-feet lining their strong eyes. They were family.

Nearly two years went by. Rena and her niece Jenna (who is the same age) were in sixth grade. The two had grown up together in Heber Valley at the base of Utah's Uintah Mountains, as had many Native Americans before them. The Ute Indians, specifically the Uintah Band, had a long history there. John Duncan had been their last great chief, and folklore held that Unca Som, a medicine man, was the oldest Indian to have lived on the reservation. Both girls were descended from these great men.

Jenna and Rena also had in common being among the first Native Americans to attend previously all-white Neola Elementary School, which happened to take a field trip to the capitol every year. Busloads of kids from their own school walked by the stone legends annually and never knew who they were. That fact nagged at Rena's heart, but what could she do?

Mr. Murray, an interested teacher from nearby Myton Elementary, became aware of Rena's frustration; he suggested the two girls journey to the state legislature and propose putting name-plates on each bust. The preteens were ecstatic. They knew what they had to do.

After numerous drafts of speeches, Rena and Jenna worked out what they would say. Their point was simple: respect. Respect John Duncan and Unca Som. Respect their historical contributions to Utah. Respect the heritage they represent. How? By acknowledging them; don't leave these men without names.

When the day came for Rena and Jenna to speak on behalf of their grandfathers, their entire families and a busload of kids from

Faith-based youth groups bring together the talents of many people to help effect change.

Myton and Neola Elementary Schools went with them for support. Both girls felt their hearts would fly from their chests when they stepped up to the microphone, but they did it. Each sixth-grader bravely testified on the floor of Utah's House of Representatives in favor of House Concurrent Resolution 7.

Rena and Jenna needn't have been so nervous. Their resolution passed both the Utah House and Senate unanimously. Nameplates were eventually engraved, and Mr. Murray helped the two girls hang them on their ancestors' statues.

For over fifty years, two solemn faces had watched over the legislative affairs of a state's capital, and no one had taken the time to find out who they were or how they had contributed to Utah's history. It took the words of two Native American youth from a rural reservation, their strong sense of ancestry, the help of one public schoolteacher, and the courage to challenge a legislative body to finally educate an entire state and bring honor to two great men and the heritage they represented.

Helping Hands

In the profiles that opened this chapter we again see very different issues and very different impacts, but the youths' respective efforts share one interesting element: family assistance. In Leonard's case, his entire family pitched in, especially his mom and dad. In Rena and Jenna's situation, it was Rena's father who first brought the issue to her attention, and both girls' entire families went with them for support when they testified in the state legislature.

Many acts of community outreach require adult guidance and help, especially in rural regions where other resources can be limited. That's okay. Look again at Leonard: his dad did the driving to deliver quilts and his mom did the bag design and much of the sewing for the first few projects.

In previous chapters, we saw Eddie borrow money from his parents; Jaclyn's mom and dad helped her set up a nonprofit organization; Hope turned to a teacher to help organize her protest against the mining practices; and school officials provided a bus. In nearly every case this book highlights, at least one teacher, parent, librarian, club supervisor, member of the clergy, organizational staff member, tribal leader, or other adult guided and equipped the youth to tackle the issues. In most cases, more than one adult got involved, but that doesn't take away from the work done by each of these kids. The grown-up help they obtained merely enabled them accomplish what they set out to do. That's a wise use of resources!

CHAPTER 4

Changing the World: Profiles of National and International Impact

"Never believe that a few caring people can't change the world for indeed, that's all who ever have."

—Margaret Mead (1901–1978), American anthropologist

Jean-Dominic (Quebec, Canada)

Ten-year-old Jean-Dominic was watching *The Simpsons* when he noticed a pearl-sized lump on his neck. He showed his mom, who wasted no time getting him to their family doctor. Within four weeks, the lump was as big as his fist. Specialists at a big-city hospital delivered the bad news: non-Hodgkin's *lymphoma* . . . the "c" word: cancer.

"There were 22 kids from Ile Bizard [Jean-Dominic's Quebec island-home] in the hospital with cancer," he recalls in a 2001 *Peace and Environmental News* article. That number seemed disproportionately high. "Being in the hospital gave me a chance to think *how did I get this cancer?*"

Jean-Dominic and his parents went to the closest public library and did their homework. What they found astounded them. Childhood cancer rates for the island were four times higher than provincial rates for Quebec, and ten times the national average. Then they found a reputable study by the National Cancer Institute (U.S.) linking non-Hodgkin's lymphoma to a commonly used *herbicide*, 2,4-D, one of the most common active ingredients in Canadian lawn-care treatments at that time.

Ile Bizard is located west of Montreal, and well over one-third of its thirteen square miles (34 square kilometers) is golf courses. Keeping *fairways* immaculate requires huge quantities of herbicides, most of which then contained 2,4-D, a substance that killed weeds like dandelions, thistles, and ragweed. Three golf courses surrounded the village Jean-Dominic called home, and all routinely used herbicides with 2,4-D. Coincidence? In Jean-Dominic's mind, no: those herbicides caused his cancer.

Even at ten years of age, Jean-Dominic knew he had to do something. With his parents' support, he organized a group of kids—as he was starting cancer treatments, no less—to gather signatures on petitions asking for herbicide and *pesticide* bans on Ile Bizard. The youngsters also picketed outside the island's town hall. Eventually, smiling and chemotherapy-bald, his face graced the front page of a major Montreal newspaper. The headline warned: "Toxic Garden."

Jean-Dominic also wrote letters to local politicians and lobbied all levels of government to prohibit the use of such chemicals on the island. After seven years of tireless effort, Jean-Dominic got the

Jean-Dominic worked to get a cancer-causing pesticide banned in his community, but the effect was nationwide.

support he needed. In 2001, the mayor of Ile Bizard enacted a ban on herbicides and pesticides for the whole island, effective immediately. Jean-Dominic was seventeen.

Other local municipalities across Canada have since passed similar laws banning herbicide and pesticide use. What of Jean-Dominic? He's now in his early twenties and is a cancer survivor. He continues to spread awareness of the health effects of using toxic chemicals in lawn care and agriculture—locally, nationally, and internationally— and his personal crusade to help his hometown has won him many awards, including one of Canada's highest honors (Canadian Order of Youth) and the United Nations Environment Award.

One determined youngster got sick, saw that his hometown were also at risk, and decided to do something about it. That's all it took to ban toxins, first on one island in Quebec, then across an entire nation.

One Step at a Time

Many people who end up impacting entire regions, even countries, didn't start out with that intent. Look at Jean-Dominic. When he started his campaign, he wanted officials to simply stop spraying his own little island with herbicides. He never imagined his protests would impact provinces across Canada, let alone other countries. Jean-Dominic just wanted a safer hometown.

Others are more intentionally ambitious, taking on world issues through international groups. (Some of those are examined in the next chapter.) Most youths, however, start with their neighborhoods, their schools, their hometowns, or with one-person-at-a-time, usually via a local club or organization. More than a few teens initially get involved simply to have fun, then gradually realize the good they're doing.

Rosemary (Pennsylvania, United States)

Rosemary is a member of 4-H. Her project area is raising and socializing Seeing Eye puppies until they're old enough to enter formal guide-dog training. That means when the puppy is about eighteen months old, Rosemary must give her dog back to the Seeing Eye organization, but it also means that about every two years she receives a new six- or seven-week-old puppy to love.

Why Youth Get Involved

One Gallup poll lists the main reasons teens themselves cite for volunteering. Not all of them are unselfish!

- compassion
- belief that they can do something for a cause about which they're passionate
- fun
- looks good on college applications and resumes
- belief that if they help others, others will help them

"I wish I could say that I first got involved with 4-H/The Seeing Eye to help the blind," she admits in a recent interview. "That would sound really good, but honestly, I always wanted to have a dog since I was little, and initially—remember, I was only eleven," she quickly adds, "the program seemed like a great way to get one."

Over the last six years, four puppies have begun their training in Rosemary's care: Logan, BeBe, Mia, and now Goldie. The little canines (cute, clumsy, round, fuzzy pups) arrive with their names, care and training instructions, a bag of food, leash and collar, and any needed medications. Each gradually starts receiving "normal" dog training (like coming when called, no jumping or begging, and housetraining). The Seeing Eye even provides specific "command words" Rosemary and her family should use during this initial training—words all program puppies need to learn. The sixteen-year-old explains:

> You know how when you have your own dog, you can let some things go? We can't do that. We have to be stricter. We train them well because we know they'll be doing a job. . . . But the main goals are socialization (you know, well-adjusted, outgoing) and manners. Except for school, we take the puppies everywhere: the post office, the library, bank, grocery store, restaurants, the dentist, and doctors' offices. That can be tricky. These dogs are not technically Seeing Eye dogs yet, so we need to ask before bringing them in.

The Seeing Eye also specifies the dogs' diets—no table scraps—and pays for everything except toys: food, vet visits, shots, medicines, even kenneling should the puppy's foster family need to go away. The participating 4-H member is responsible for tracking such expenses and maintaining additional records for things like health and weight.

Rosemary says, "We learn responsibility raising the dogs, and it's fun." Rosemary's mom adds that the kids also learn economics, record keeping, and discipline through this project. "The biggest challenge is giving them up," Rosemary replies when asked what challenges she's encountered raising guide dogs:

> But after they finish formal training, the dogs do what's called a "town walk" [where the dogs and their handlers navigate real sidewalks, intersections, and people] to which we're invited as observers, so we get to see our dogs at work. I got to see BeBe with an actual blind person, and that's cool.
>
> The Seeing Eye also holds an annual family-day picnic where puppy foster families get to hear blind people speak about their dogs and what the program has done for them. It's then that you realize what you're doing. It's really nice to hear how these dogs are changing lives.

Only about 50 or 60 percent of the trainees make the cut. In fact, only one of Rosemary's three dogs became an official Seeing Eye

The Seeing Eye program trains dogs that will later assist vision-impaired persons.

Rosemary and her current trainee, Goldie

dog; that was BeBe. Logan went on to work customs at an airport, and a family adopted Mia. (As of this writing, Rosemary is still working with Goldie.)

"You don't get to communicate with the new owners directly, but you do hear general things. We learned that BeBe went to a blind attorney in a big city. BeBe helps her walk to her office and the courthouse every day. That's cool."

Varying Results

Clearly how rural youths impact lives and causes varies. Jean-Dominic ended up changing not only his local government's view of herbicides, but his province, country, and other nations as well; he

Fun Facts

What do two U.S. first ladies, a vice president, at least four NASA astronauts, one NASCAR champion, a Heisman Trophy winner, the creator of Garfield, countless country singers, Michael Jackson's brother, a Metropolitan Opera star, and a host of TV and film stars have in common? They were all members of 4-H! (Jacqueline Kennedy-Onassis and Roslyn Carter; Al Gore; NASA's Bonnie Dunbar, Ellison Onizuka, Jerry Ross, and Alan Shepard; NASCAR's Ned Jarrett; the NFL's Herschel Walker; Garfield's Jim Davis; country music's Faith Hill, Martina McBride, Johnny Cash, Lionel Cartwright, Dolly Parton, and others; Jermaine Jackson; opera singer Sherill Milnes; and entertainment's Johnny Carson, Sissy Spacek, Holly Hunter, and others)

indirectly helped thousands of people. And he did it largely on his own. That's dramatic.

Rosemary's impact is more subtle. She's changing lives one person at a time through her dogs. In just her tri-county area, three 4-H/The Seeing Eye Puppy Clubs exist, each hosting twenty to twenty-five puppies at a time. That means every wave of new dogs can potentially impact dozens of visually impaired people and others across the continent, but the work starts with one youth paired with a single puppy. And Rosemary can do that with the help of two national programs (4-H and The Seeing Eye).

A Small World

Other teens set their sights a bit farther from home. One morning at church, Kristin and Kyle heard of the plight of AIDS orphans in Zambia, Africa. Orphan schools were springing up in that nation faster than supplies could support them, and these siblings wanted to help. But how? A ministry located in Zambia guided them regarding the greatest needs, and with the support of their home church, the ministry in Africa, and a team of four other families, fifteen-year-old Kristin and her twelve-year-old brother were on a plane within the year. They didn't go empty-handed.

First, the siblings emptied their local dollar store's supply of antibiotic ointment, **hydrocortisone** cream, adhesive bandages, toothbrushes, and toothpaste. They also bought school supplies, books, jump ropes, and soccer balls with their own money. Then they raided their own closets and thrift shops for children's clothing to share. With five families and nineteen team members gathering similar supplies, you can imagine how much luggage this group took. Getting needed items to desperate schools was a huge part of their trip.

"Our team was distributing supplies to one of the orphan's schools we visited," Kristin shares. "Hundreds of dusty, barefoot boys and girls sat crammed together on a clay floor. As we handed their teachers each item, the children clapped." She pauses. "In our country, the loudest applause would have been for things like soccer balls. Do you know what these kids cheered the loudest for? *Toothpaste* and a bag of plain *rolls*—they would eat that day."

The team of families also took music and training skills. Music **pervades** African culture. When you can't speak Bemba, you can communicate in song. Kristin took her flute; other teens took guitars and two keyboards, one of which Kyle used to teach the orphans new music. At the end of the two camps the youths ran, they left the keyboards with the schools.

Kristin did her part to change the world by making a difference in the lives of these children from Zambia.

"We take so much for granted here," observes Kyle. "I never realized I had so much."

Kristin and Kyle had the support of two faith-based organizations, members of their local church, their parents, and dozens of friends and family. Consequently, these two were fortunate to be able to set foot on the foreign soil they longed to help. Living in a rural township was irrelevant. Other kids have reached across the ocean less directly.

One eleven-year-old from Washington State wanted to help victims of the December 2004 tsunami that crashed into Southeast Asia. He wasn't old enough to have a job, but he could make and sell hot chocolate during the Northwest's cold winter days. His hot-chocolate stand raised $225, which he donated to tsunami relief.

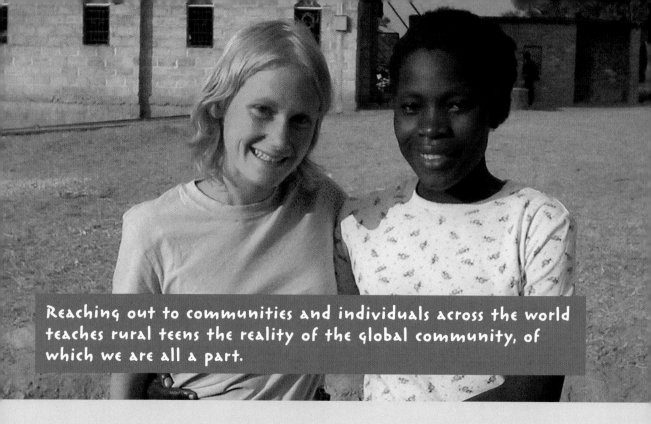

Reaching out to communities and individuals across the world teaches rural teens the reality of the global community, of which we are all a part.

Joint Effort

Generally, reaching out to communities across your nation or the world requires the assistance of well-connected national and international organizations. They've already navigated government systems and bureaucracy; they know where the greatest needs are and how to reach them; and most organizations are just dying for help. Some of the more well-know national and international charitable or activist groups include:

- Amnesty International

- AmeriCorps

- CARE

- Christian Children's Fund

- Compassion International

- Greenpeace

- Habitat for Humanity

- Heifer Project International

- Nature Conservancy

- Peace Corps

- Red Cross

- Salvation Army

- Save the Children

- Sierra Club

- Special Olympics

- United Nations Volunteers

- Volunteers for Peace

- WorldPeace Camp

- Youth Volunteer Corps

Most of these organizations have both Canadian and U.S. chapters.

Countless faith-based groups, missions organizations, and community- and school-based clubs also offer opportunities for national and international service. A few offer the experience as a kind of summer camp. Many also have funding, grants, and scholarships available, and make all the arrangements. These groups just need your hands and mind—and perhaps most important, your heart.

Spotlight: 4-H

Local, state, provincial, and national 4-H groups abound throughout North America. In 2002, Canada boasted over 2,400 active clubs with 32,870 combined members; in 2003, the United States cited over 1.5 million active members spread over 89,636 clubs.

To understand 4-H, it's helpful to trace its rural roots. 4-H didn't really start in one time or place. In the late 1800s, agricultural colleges across the United States were simultaneously doing a great deal of work to specifically improve farming, but many farmers were resistant to advancements, preferring traditional ways. Researchers needed a way to get their discoveries into use.

Who better to try something new than young people? Many states began exploring agricultural youth programs just prior to 1900: "Boys' Corn Clubs" and "Girls' Canning Clubs" for instance. When parents saw how much more efficient and productive new hybrid seeds, techniques, or tools were (as their offspring experimented with them), they realized the value of such innovations, so rural youth programs became the primary vehicle for introducing new farm technology to adults.

The earliest such youth program on record is one A. B. Graham started in Ohio in 1902. Some consider it the birthplace of 4-H USA, but many such boys' and girls' clubs were springing up across the nation.

In addition to getting technology to rural farms, these clubs sought to help young people develop "not by means of the three R's, but rather by the means of the three H's—heads, hearts, and hands." It wasn't until 1911, when club leaders gathered for a national meeting in Washington, that the fourth H appeared.

Accounts differ. Some credit O. H. Benson with suggesting the addition of "health" to "resist disease, enjoy life, and make for efficiency." Others credit O. B. Martin, who was directing club work in the South. Most, though, do agree that O. H. Benson first suggested the fourth H stand for "hustle!" It didn't fly.

U.S. club representatives adopted the official name "4-H" (head, heart, hands, and health) and the four-leaf-clover design at that 1911 gathering. Although similar Canadian youth programs called Boys' and Girls' Clubs began officially in Manitoba just two years earlier, Canada did not adopt the 4-H name until 1952 and is still not affiliated directly with the U.S. program. In fact, the two countries use different mottos—Canada: "to learn by doing"; the U.S.: "to make the best better." Both employ the official 4-H pledge.

By the mid-1900s, many families were leaving farm life for jobs in the city. The needs of urban and suburban youth differed from those of rural youth, so 4-H expanded to adapt to those needs. Today's 4-H is very different from the clubs of the early 1900s, but the goal of the organization has remained unchanged: to help young people develop life skills through specific project work. With nearly 100 project areas from which to choose, from animals to the environment and from performing arts to science or technology, 4-H members can literally design their own club experience.

CHAPTER 5
Championing the Cause:
Profiles of Issue-Specific Impact

"Needs that make you weep or pound the table awaken and unlock your creativity."

—Bobb Biehl, from *The On My Own Handbook: 100 Secrets of Success to Prepare Young People for Life in the Real World*

Stephanie (Minnesota, United States)

"Years ago doctors wondered if I'd ever be able to take a step on my own," this teenager explains in an interview for America's Promise: The Alliance for Youth:

Without expensive treatments, I faced being crippled because of a genetic birth defect. Without hesitation, the Shriners stepped in to make a difference in my life. For sixteen years, Shriners [Hospital] provided me with countless treatments, surgeries, and ankle and food braces, all free of cost. Today I am able to take steps on my own because of the generosity and compassion of the Shriners.

I wanted to give back to the hospital, so in 2000 I started a fundraiser in my community that would benefit the hospital. . . . The event is a motorcycle ride called the Ride for Shrine. It's very close to my heart.

I plan and organize the event myself. I book the *venue*, obtain donated food and beverages from local businesses, design and print all posters, banners, waivers, and tickets, and also get local businesses to donate raffle prizes. . . . It's not always easy to get others involved, but it will happen. Be persistent and be confident—it makes it harder for people to say no when you ask them to get involved.

I also take care of advertising the event on radio, television, and in the newspapers. This event takes an entire year worth of planning, and I am more than happy to do all of it. . . . The Ride for Shrine is my passion. I believe that by holding the event, I am making the world a better place for all of us.

Shriners Hospitals for Children is a network of twenty-two pediatric hospitals specializing in *orthopedics*, burns, and spinal cord injuries. Its medical services are totally free of charge to any child under the age of eighteen. Shriners Hospitals are located throughout North America. Millions of children and teens—like Stephanie—have been helped.

Eddie (Wyoming, United States)

This Native American youth was only a high-school sophomore when a wave of suicides struck the reservation where he lived—ten

Organizing a marathon or race is one way rural teens can raise money or awareness for an important cause.

suicides, all young people, all from Wyoming's Wind River Reservation, all Native American.

"It was just a really bad time," Eddie recalls in the *Scholastic Update* article "Armed with Idealism: Teen Volunteers" by Donna Larson, James Earl Hardy, Lauren Tarshis, Leah Eskin, and Phil Sudo. "Sad scary."

Determined to curb the suicides impacting the Arapahoe and Shoshone tribes who lived there, reservation leaders called on an outside Native American organization for guidance. The result was Youth Council. This council offered a safe place for local teens to express their feelings, hammer out issues unique to reservation life,

and work together to find solutions. It also organized sports clinics, exhibits, and outings.

"I remember thinking the idea wouldn't work," continues Eddie, who prior to joining Youth Council was often drunk and frequently cut classes, "but when I started going to meetings, I started feeling more confidence in myself."

It didn't take long for club members to recognize Eddie's potential and elect him president. That was the opportunity he needed. Under Eddie's inspiration and leadership, Youth Council reclaimed a nearby abandoned field upon which they constructed an authentic Native American village designed to stir tribal pride, educate the public, and attract tourism. The completed village now employs

Time after Time

- U.S. teen-volunteers averaged thirty-nine hours of service per year in 2004, or approximately one hour per week throughout the school year.

- On average, Canadian youth-volunteers invested 130 hours per year helping others. That's two to three hours per week!

reservation teens, holds cultural demonstrations for tourists (including dance, folklore, cooking, and crafts), and sells reservation products like jewelry, pottery, and weavings.

Youth Council turned Eddie's life around. He stopped cutting classes and ultimately entered the University of Wyoming. The U.S. Congress even asked him to testify about Indian Issues. "I started feeling really good that I was doing something that would help make a better way of life for the Indian people," Eddie continues. "Now we have a purpose."

Ryan (Ontario, Canada)

When six-year-old Ryan heard his first-grade teacher, Mrs. Prest, talk about African people who didn't have clean water, he begged his mom and dad to give him extra chores so he could earn enough money to drill a well in Africa. He worked for four months to earn seventy dollars. With the help of his classmates, he went on to raise the rest of the $2,000 needed for the well.

Spotlight: Aboriginal and Native American Youth Councils

Unlike many organizations in this book, the term "Youth Council" refers more to a concept than a single, governing organization. Individual tribes can establish independent youth councils like Arizona's Akimel O'odham/Pee-Posh Youth Council (Gila River Indian Community). Entire states or provinces can create regional youth councils as Manitoba did through Manitoba First Nation Youth Council. Other youth councils are nationwide, such as the United States' National Indian Youth Council founded in 1961 in Gallup, New Mexico.

Whether its affiliated with an independent, local tribal group or tied to a larger organization, the concept of Youth Council is the same: ensuring Native American and Aboriginal youths opportunities to participate in and become assets to their communities. Youth Council is about young people having a voice in matters concerning them; it's about Native American teens helping others and bettering their regions; it's about Aboriginal youths gaining experience and developing leadership skills; it is also about kids having fun.

Ryan's efforts didn't stop there. Eventually his work caught the attention of the media and the support of many nonprofit organizations (such as WaterCan, Canadian Physicians for Aid and Relief, and Free the Children). His foundation, Ryan's Well, soon raised nearly $1 million to get clean water to people half a world away.

Ryan is now a teenager, and his fundraising continues. He has spoken to thousands of students across North America about Africa's plight. He has appeared on television and radio and has been featured by many newspapers and magazines including *Reader's Digest*. Most important, many Africans can thank Ryan for wells that provide them with fresh water.

Broken Hearts

In each of these three cases, something deeply moved the youth. Whether from personal experience or compassion from afar, it was Eddie's, Stephanie's, and Ryan's wrenching emotions that moved them. Passion can be a powerful force.

Yes, a few teens get involved for selfish reasons—what they can get out of it—but far more are genuinely driven by deep feelings. Here are just a few more examples:

- One group of eighth-grade students at a rural West Virginia middle school were so moved by the events they saw unfolding on September 11, 2001, they decided to ask each eighth-grader *in the state* to donate $1 to the rebuilding of the Pentagon. They collected over $5,000, and every cent went directly to the rebuilding effort.

- When visiting Jamaica, one fourteen-year-old was stunned to learn of the technology void in island schools. The school Anders visited did have a computer: one computer for 850 kids. This young man was so touched that within two short years, by the time he was sixteen, Anders had established his own nonprofit organization, Teens for Technology, and set up computer labs in over 100 Jamaican schools.

- Kate loves animals. Her heart holds a particular soft spot for homeless or abandoned ones, but caring for them and finding placements costs money she doesn't have. Her solution? Pennies for Pets—a fundraising drive she conducted at her local school. Every cent went to the animals. Her efforts and compassion earned special recognition from the National Association for Humane and Environmental Education's Humane Teen program. But that's not why Kate did it. She did it out of love.

- Another teen was so heartbroken when she heard a regional newscast about a police dog being shot that she came up with something similar: Pennies to Protect Police Dogs. The idea was to collect people's spare change to buy bulletproof vests for the canines. Thanks to her effort, more than 200 dogs across the continent have protective vests, at a pricey $600 each. Stacey's pennies led to more than $200,000 for the dogs.

- At age nine, one Florida girl felt so sorry for a balding chemotherapy patient she saw that she started collecting hats for pediatric cancer patients. Since then, Mollie has collected over 10,000 hats donated by classmates, various organizations, athletes, and even sports teams. She calls her program Hats for Kids.

- Struck by the level of local poverty and hunger, one group of North Carolina teens held a community breakfast to raise money for the hungry in their region. The cash bought boxes of groceries to deliver to needy households.

Perhaps the most effective community action is born of such emotions, but every heartbreak doesn't require starting your own foundation or going nationwide. Needs exist in your own backyard, and there are numerous ways to help. Assist a handicapped or elderly person with physical chores. Babysit for a single parent. Take

Make a
difference:
get involved!

Five "Gets" of Getting Involved

Get Inspired: Notice. Pay Attention. Observe. Feel!

Get Information: Use your mind to respond to feelings. Let your heartbreak, compassion, frustration, competitiveness, or outrage drive you to learn more. Dig through books, newspapers, journals, magazine articles, reports, and the Internet for related information. (Use your school or public libraries.) Find out what others tried, what worked, what didn't, and why. Talk with people. Ask questions. Finally, don't think every need has to be huge or complex and requires a ton of research. Sometimes gathering information is as simple as asking a needy person when a good time to get together might be.

Get Creative: Use passion to fuel your energy and knowledge to stimulate creativity. Someone once said, "Necessity is the mother of invention." That's absolutely true. If you see a need, whether individual or communitywide, and some form of passion fuels an inner drive to fill that need, you'll invent a way to do just that! Think it through. How can you apply the information you researched to your unique cause and its unique circumstances? What will work for you?

Get Equipped: Once you've figured out a plausible plan of action, it's time to gather what you'll need to facilitate it: materials (supplies), manpower (any people you need to help), time, and services (transportation, mailing, Web site, etc.). Perhaps the most important tool to prepare—and many people (youths and adults alike) forget this—is you. Anyone who wants to effectively make a difference needs to equip his heart, mind, and body. Activism drains even the most selfless, driven people—emotionally, mentally, and physically. Don't neglect to take care of yourself while you're trying to care for others!

Get Going: Finally, take all that inspiration, information, those creative solutions, and their means and do something. Put all that heart and planning into action.

firewood to a needy family without heat. Visit a senior citizen or shut-in. Write a letter of gratitude to a soldier far from home. Volunteer to work with kids in your community through sports, reading, or the arts. Take in a stray cat. Pick up litter along local roads or in creeks. The possibilities are endless.

Join the Crowd

Today's youth often gets a bad rap. Many adults think twenty-first century teens are spoiled, slow to learn, quickly bored, and self-centered. Yet consider the words of one editorial by Christina Hoff Sommers, as quoted in *American Values: Opposing Viewpoints:*

> There is a great deal of simple good-heartedness, instinctive fair-mindedness, and spontaneous generosity of spirit in our young people. . . . They are donating blood to the Red Cross in record numbers. They deliver food to housebound elderly people. They spend part of their summer vacation working with deaf children or doing volunteer work in Mexico. This is a generation of kids that is doing some very concrete and effective things for other people.

Nearly one-third of all North American youths (U.S. and Canadian) gave of themselves in 2004 in some capacity: time, talents, or treasures. How you get involved is perhaps less important than the fact that you get involved. Whether you call your home urban, suburban, or rural, don't let any obstacles keep you from doing the good you were meant to do. These rural youths didn't, and despite the odds, they're making a difference.

Further Reading

Adolph, Val, and Valerie Ahwee. *Making a Difference: A Guide to Volunteering for Canadian Youth*. Toronto, Ont.: Summerhill Pr. Ltd., 2000.

Blaustein, Arthur I. *Make a Difference: America's Guide to Volunteering and Community Service*. Berkeley, Calif.: Heyday Books, 2002.

Brain, Marshall. *A Teenager's Guide to the Real World*. Raleigh, N.C.: BYG Publishing Inc., 1997.

Coplin, William D. *How You Can Help: An Easy Guide to Incorporating Good Deeds into Everyday Life*. New York: Routledge, 2000.

Halpin, Mikki. *It's Your World—If You Don't Like It, Change It: Activism for Teenagers*. New York: Simon Pulse, 2004.

Koch, Carl. *I Know Things Now: Stories by Teenagers* 1. Winona, Minn.: Saint Mary's Press, 1996.

Lewis, Barbara A. *Kids with Courage: True Stories About Young People Making a Difference*. Minneapolis, Minn.: Free Spirit Publishing, Inc., 2002.

Lewis, Barbara A., and Pamela Espeland. *The Kid's Guide to Service Projects: Over 500 Service Ideas for Young People Who Want to Make a Difference*. Minneapolis, Minn.: Free Spirit Publishing, Inc., 1995.

Lewis, Barbara A., and Pamela Espeland. *What Do You Stand for? A Kid's Guide to Building Character*. Minneapolis, Minn.: Free Spirit Publishing, 1997.

Lewis, Barbara A., Pamela Espeland, and Caryn Pernu. *The Kid's Guide to Social Action: How to Solve the Social Problems You Choose and Turn Creative Thinking Into Positive Action*. Minneapolis, Minn.: Free Spirit Publishing, Inc., 1998.

Kielburger, Craig, and Kevin Major. *Free the Children: A Young Man Fights Against Child Labor and Proves That Children Can Change the World*. New York: Harper Perennial, 1999.

Kielburger, Marc, and Craig Kielburger. *Take Action! A Guide to Active Citizenship*. Hoboken, N.J.: John Wiley and Sons, Inc., 2002.

Salzman, Marian, and Teresa Reisgies. *150 Ways Teens Can Make a Difference: A Handbook for Action*. Princeton, N.J.: Peterson's Guides, Inc., 2001.

For More Information

4-H
www.4h-usa.org (U.S.)
www.4-h-canada.ca (Canada)

America's Promise: The Alliance for Youth
www.americaspromise.org

AmeriCorps
www.americorps.org

Best Buddies International
www.bestbuddies.org

Big Brothers Big Sisters
www.bbbsa.org (U.S.)
www.bbbsc.ca (Canada)

Boys' and Girls' Clubs
www.bgca.org (of America)
www.bgccan.com (of Canada)

Canadian 4-H Council
930 Carling Avenue, Bldg. #26
Ottawa, Ontario K1A 0C6
613.234.4448
www.4-h-canada.ca/index.html

Canadian Rural Information Center
(Entrepreneurship and Opportunities for Rural Youth)
www.rural.gc.ca/cris/youth/index_e.phtml

Cultivating Peace (Canada) – Students – Organizations to Join
www.cultivatingpeace.ca/students/organizations.html

Interact Clubs (Rotary International)
www.rotary6060.org/interact.htm

Key Club International (Kiwanis International)
www.keyclub.org

Leo Clubs (Lions Clubs International)
www.lionsclubs.org/EN/content/youth_leo_clubs.shtml

Network for Good
www.networkforgood.org

Rural Assistance Center
www.raconline.org/info_guides

Rural School and Community Trust
www.ruraledu.org

Scouting
www.girlguides.ca (Girl Guides of Canada)
www.girlscouts.org (Girl Scouts of the U.S.A.)
www.scouting.org (Boy Scouts of America)
www.scouts.ca (Boy Scouts of Canada)
www.wagggsworld.org (World Association of Girl Guides and Girl Scouts)

The Teenager's Guide to the Real World Online
(20 Ways for Teenagers to Help Other People Volunteering)
www.bygpub.com/books/tg2rw/volunteer.html

Teens Act Out
www.caprojectlean.org/teensactout/makedifference/default.asp

What Kids Can Do, Inc
PO Box 603252
Providence, RI 02906
401.247.7665
www.whatkidscando.org

YMCA
www.ymca.net (US)
www.ymca.ca.eng_abouty.htm

YOUCAN—Youth Canada Association
www.youcan.ca

Youth Activism Project
www.youthactivism.com

Youth Service America
www.ysa.org
www.servenet.org

Youth Venture
www.youthventure.org

Publisher's note:
The Web sites listed on this page were active at the time of publication. The publisher is not responsible for Web sites that have changed their addresses or discontinued operation since the date of publication. The publisher will review and update the Web-site list upon each reprint.

Glossary

Aboriginal: A member of any of the peoples that are descended from the original inhabitants of an area, such as the peoples who inhabited Canada before the arrival of European settlers.

encampment: A place occupied by a camp.

fairways: The closely mown area on a golf hole that forms the main avenue between a tee and a green.

herbicide: A chemical preparation designed to kill plants.

hydrocortisone: A synthetic steroid used to treat inflammatory and allergic conditions.

initiative: The first step in a process that determines subsequent events.

lymphoma: A malignant tumor originating in a lymph node.

orthopedics: The branch of medicine concerned with the nature and correction of disorders of the bones, joints, ligaments, and muscles.

pervades: Spreads throughout.

pesticide: A chemical substance used to kill pests, especially insects.

revitalization: The process of giving new life to something.

radicals: People whose behavior is marked by extreme departures from what is usual or traditional.

saturate: To fill something so completely nothing else can be added.

stereotypes: Judgments and generalizations based on inaccurate and incomplete information.

venue: A place where an event occurs, especially a sporting event or concert.

Index

Picture Credits

Corel: p. 56
Ford, Jean: pp. 68, 71, 72
Fotolia Images: pp. 36, 43
iStock: pp. 9, 16, 19, 33, 42, 48, 51, 58, 60, 76
    Brandenburg, Dan: p. 35
    Creach, Alan: p. 27
    Grove, Bill: p. 31
    Mitic, Slobo: p. 21
    Turay, Lisa: p. 24
    Viisimaa, Peeter: p. 12
    Whaley, Jerry: p. 29
    Widling, Philippe: p. 11
Jupiter Images: pp. 63, 79
Phoenixpix: p. 39
Seeing Eye: p. 67
Stockbyte: p. 52
USDA, Ken Hammond: pp. 80, 85

To the best knowledge of the publisher, all other images are in the public domain. If any image has been inadvertently uncredited, please notify Harding House Publishing Service, Vestal, New York 13850, so that rectification can be made for future printings.

Biographies

Author

Jean Otto Ford was born and raised in rural, northern Pennsylvania where dusty roads, country fairs, and "nothin'-to-do-on-a-Saturday-night" shaped her youth. She experienced firsthand the positive impact teens had on her community then, and living in a small town now, she continues to see the impact rural kids can have not just in their community, in the region, and even across the world.

Ford is a freelance author, writer, artist, and public speaker residing in Perkasie, Pennsylvania, with her husband, two teenage children, and dog, Gracie. *Teens Who Make a Difference in Rural Communities: Youth Outreach Organizations and Community Action* is the tenth educational title she has written for Mason Crest.

Series Consultant

Celeste J. Carmichael is a 4-H Youth Development Program Specialist at the Cornell University Cooperative Extension Administrative Unit in Ithaca, New York. She provides leadership to statewide 4-H Youth Development efforts including communications, curriculum, and conferences. She communicates the needs and impacts of the 4-H program to staff and decision makers, distributing information about issues related to youth and development, such as trends for rural youth.